S0-AZY-965

THE MOUND BUILDERS

Meridel Le Sueur

THE MOUND BUILDERS

←A FIRST BOOK→
Franklin Watts, Inc.
New York, 1974

Picture research by Selma Hamdan
Map by George Buctel

Illustration credits

Ohio Historical Society pp. ii, viii, 4, 7, 8, 13 (2), 31, 44, 45, 46; National Park Service, U.S. Department of the Interior pp. 9, 18, 36, 38, 39, 40, 41, 42, 47; Museum of the American Indian p. 32; Museum of Primitive Art, New York pp. 52, 53; Minnesota Historical Society p. 50.

Library of Congress Cataloging in Publication Data

Le Sueur, Meridel.
    The mound builders.

    (A First book)
    SUMMARY: Describes various ancient mound-building cultures from the evidence found in surviving mounds and their contents.
    Bibliography: p.
    1. Mound-builders—Juvenile literature. [1. Mound builders. 2. Mounds] I. Title.
E73.L4   913'.031   73-22497
ISBN 0-531-02717-1

Copyright © 1974 by Franklin Watts, Inc.
Printed in the United States of America
6 5 4 3 2 1

Clark Branch

APR 14 1975

CJ
407.
3
L565M

75- 34682 A19

Cleveland Public Library

Flight over Time
and Space 1

Up the Down Staircase 11

Dark Ancestors 17

Food Gatherers—
Flower People 21

The Dead and the Living 23

Poverty Point's
Great Pyramids 27

Adena Mounds of the Dead 29

Hopewell Merchants
of America 35

The Artistic Mississippians 49

The Silent Heritage 55

Bibliography 57

Index 59

contents

For Beth Dora, Benjamin,
Gabriel and
all the Flower Children

THE MOUND BUILDERS

If you could step into a time machine, go back a thousand years, and fly over the Americas, beginning in Peru, passing over Mexico, crossing the Gulf of Mexico, and flying up the mouth of the Mississippi as far north as the states of Ohio, Illinois, and Wisconsin, you would be able to look down on settlements around immense pyramids, larger than those found in Egypt.

Today, these centers and their grandiose monuments exist as mounds, found across the face of the American continent. There are thousands of them, from as far east as Florida. They follow the course of the great mid-American rivers as far west as the Rockies. The ancient people who built these structures existed before the Indians as we now know them, and were the forerunners of these later Indians.

They left these mounds as messages, as monuments to their primitive civilization.

From your flying time machine, you would be filled with awe as you looked down and saw the huge temples, sometimes as many as a hundred smaller ones clustered around the larger ones, leading into plazas where thousands of people could meet together, with intricate ramps leading to river landings, and into villages with thatched roofs, clustered together into groups. You could see giant bird effigies, processions oriented toward the

flight over time and space

sun, moon, or stars, thousands of people in bright woven fabrics coming in flowered barges up the Mississippi or down the Wisconsin and Illinois to meet at the summer solstice to celebrate with dance, music, and prayer. Some would be in masks of obsidian with antlers of elk, dancing with drums and rattles, coming to the blazing ceremonial fires at the apex of the pyramids. These silent structures with their animal and bird effigies speak to us of pre-American history, of a large and vigorous civilization.

These mounds — as high, some of them, as the pyramids in Egypt — are entirely made of earth, tamped down over wooden structures, funeral pyres with steps outside leading straight up to the flattened tops which must have had temples on them. This earth must have been carried by hand by thousands of men, women, and children in earthen baskets, and laid down without any of the tools we have today. They built the mounds in perfect circles, squares, octagons, ellipses. It is estimated that one contains as much as 21,690,000 cubic feet of soil. How many baskets of soil would that be?

To take some examples of mounds, in Cahokia Mounds State Park on the Mississippi River in the state of Illinois, there is a pyramid a hundred feet high, covering sixteen acres of ground, seen in splendor as it rises from the surrounding plains. There are forty mound structures in the Cahokia Park alone. These mounds are the largest temple mounds in North America, the largest earthen structures north of Mexico. The Great Serpent Mound of Adams County, Ohio, is 1,254 feet long, 20 feet wide, and 5 feet high. Shaped like a serpent, it is the largest serpent effigy in the world.

There are many thousands of sites of these mounds — ten thousand in the Ohio Valley alone. The most extensive now remaining are those at Poverty Point in Louisiana. One mound is

700 feet by 800 feet and 70 feet high. Here the complex villages cluster along a street with a pyramid at each end upon which temples once existed where the priest or shaman lived and worshipped.

The conical mounds at Poverty Point were probably funeral mounds. There are also enormous arrangements of octagons; the outer one of six concentric forms is three-quarters of a mile in diameter. It is thought that the conical structures may be the oldest of the mounds.

The structures at Cahokia indicate an immense ceremonial center. On the Little Miami River in Ohio, there is a walled embankment up to 20 feet high, faced with stone lacings, along an irregular plateau 230 feet above the flood plain, with a palisade whose gates open into an immense earth stockade a mile long north to south, three times the length of the wall.

At Marietta on the Muskingum was the religious center of the Hopewellian people (c. 400 B.C. — 900 A.D.). There are two rectangular earthworks here, enclosed areas of forty acres and one of twenty-seven within an embankment which is 25,000 square feet at the base and from four to ten feet high. There are four flat-topped pyramids within the forty-acre area. They probably had wooden temples on top. There is a graded pathway leading to the river which may have been a formal road for visitors disembarking for ceremonials.

At one time the mounds contained treasures, but much has been destroyed by treasure hunters and the old methods of digging or even dynamiting or bulldozing. Incredible treasures were unearthed in the Scioto Valley near Chillicothe, Ohio. They were taken from elongated sepulchre vaults 250 feet wide, 150 feet long, and 25 feet high. In these were found dead men buried in their finery. They were placed atop a platform of logs with their tools and ornaments beside them for use in the next world.

Twenty gallons of river pearls were found in a single grave. Some graves indicate the nature of their society. Chiefs, priests, and noblemen were buried with jewelry of bone shale, stone necklaces indicating highly developed lapidary art. Breastplates, headdresses, ornaments of mica were found with colored, handsomely woven cloth around the corpses. Some mounds contained a single body, others had dozens or more, and some seemed to be mass burials or cremations or burials of defleshed bones.

Some of the mounds were undoubtedly burial mounds, built by the ancestors of the Indians as we now know them. They, the mound builders, were a people who learned to gather food, and much later to do some farming. They could bury their dead, develop a society, and build monuments such as these mounds to immortality. They accumulated wealth also. The Hopewellian Mounds of Ohio show that they were traders, obtaining mica, pearl, and copper. Ceremonial axes have been found, carvings of antler and bone, and hammered silver, obsidian jewelry, sharks' teeth, turtle shells, and flints that must have come from as far west as Dakota or even Montana. Pottery with designs like those of the Aztecs have been found, exquisitely colored cloth, and obsidian masks.

But who were these people? Where did they come from? Why did they build these mounds? And where did they go? These ruins are a mystery.

A copper breastplate
with a conventional
cut-out design.
Hopewell culture.

There are many opinions and theories, some of which have changed entirely in the last ten years. Where did these first Americans come from? Some say over the Bering Strait, over the top of the world. Others say they came from the south, across the Gulf and up the rivers. Periods of time are also in dispute, although there is agreement that the mound builders date back to 1000 B.C. The most spectacular era was from the sixth to the fourteenth century A.D., and the last mounds were built in the seventeenth or eighteenth century.

The answers will have to be "dug" for by future archaeologists and anthropologists. The mounds speak a message we are just beginning to read.

Artifacts from the Hopewell mounds in Ohio.
Page 7: an obsidian knife blade.
Page 8: a vessel with a duck design.
Page 9: a bird-shaped artifact.

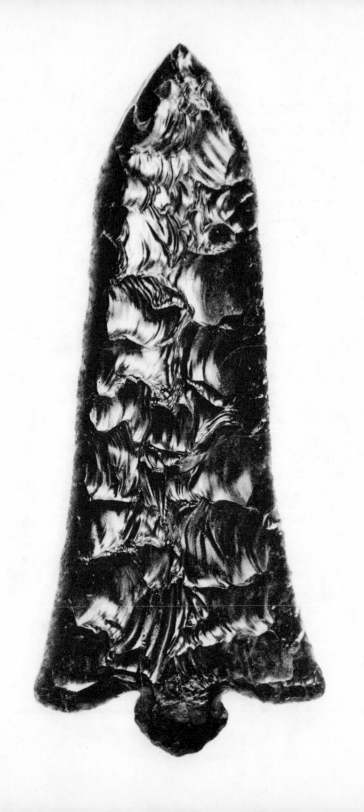

The mystery of the mounds has been, since De Soto first saw them, a part of the romance of prehistoric America. They are purely American, not found anywhere else — our antiques, our ruins.

Theories were advanced of a people escaping from the Tower of Babel, or of the lost Israelite tribe of Dan. Some thought vagrant Scandinavian fishermen landed at Greenland. Others believed that the Druid Irish brought their magic circles as far west as the Teton Mountains. An Ignatius Donnelly wrote a book saying the mound builders were from the lost continent of Atlantis. The Indians also had myths of leaving a burning continent in small curraghs and landing on the Atlantic Coast of an ancient America. There were also tales of Behemoth, a monster mammoth who destroyed the mound builders, and European myths of lands ravaged by dragons or freed by St. George.

In 1796 a writer, Francis Baily, came with settlers down the Ohio and saw the barrows, tumuli (burial mounds) of the great mound earthworks, and even then noted that the graves had been raided, bones and pottery stolen. He said about them: "They were built by a race of people more enlightened than the present Indians, and at some period of time very far distant; for

up the down staircase

the present Indians know nothing about their use, nor have they any tradition concerning them."

Thomas Jefferson's investigation of a mound in Virginia was the first scientific dig in North America. Jefferson conducted the excavation, being careful not to destroy artifacts and to keep a written record.

Scientists and philosophers of the last century were moved by the sight of the Great Serpent Mound in Ohio and Poverty Point along the Mississippi, which seemed to be witnesses to a vanished civilization. They assumed that these civilizations came from Asia, across the Bering Strait, or across a land bridge now gone, reaching down from Siberia.

Another argument suggests that a corridor was opened up by the Wisconsin glacier, fifteen thousand years before the stone spear hunters appeared. This corridor has yielded no sign of their passing. Who was going up the corridor and who was coming down? And when?

How recently did they come up or down the river, over the Strait, down over the top of America or up from South America? Did they originate in Africa or Asia? When did they come here and where did they come from?

The Bering Strait is fifty-six miles across today. In winter it freezes over. It is established that four times glaciers descended over the continent with one hundred fifty to three hundred thousand year periods of warmth in between.

Two nineteenth-century plans of the Seip Mound group in Ohio.

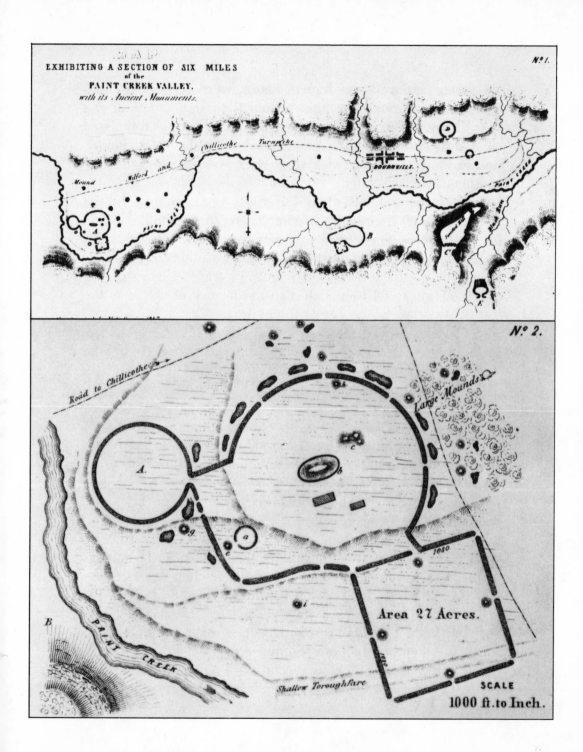

Some extremists say human beings were here thirty thousand years ago. Some say three or four thousand. The skull of a man discovered in Florida early in 1973 has been reliably dated as at least ten thousand years old, making it the oldest human find in the eastern United States. Most experts agree that the continent was populated by 1500 B.C.

There are no fossils of apes. Earliest American man did not differ too much from living species. There appears to be no record of the transition from ape to man as on other continents. No transitional types have been discovered. Two hundred skulls of human beings have been found, but not one of them suggests any evolution from prehuman man to the present, either in the form of the skull or the size of the brain.

There is the excavated finding of the Clovis, New Mexico, spear points dated twelve thousand years ago. There are the Folsom points found in the Sandia Mountains of New Mexico. These flint points are delicately made with various methods and skills. Their makers must have known the outcrops of flint all over the country. They had to have a refined and sharp flint to pierce the thick hides of the mammoths and big-horned bisons they hunted. They made the spear points hard as steel, using quality flint.

They were rovers, hunters of the big animals of the plains, spear throwers. It was this invention, the stone projectile point, which made them the hunters they were and enabled them to survive. They were apparently self-reliant nomads. Their tools were the hide-scraper flint knives and the chopper, a heavy-edged stone hand axe. The flint was fire-hardened to pierce the heavy skin of the beasts.

The finding of these distinctive stone tools and flints as far south as Argentina sharpens the question. Did early man come down or did he go up? How recently did he come down, if he did, over the top of the world? How could such a slow flow of people, endangered by climate and enormous mammoths, filter down as ice floes melted? Are today's Eskimos the sole survivors of what are called the Paleo (or ancient) hunters?

Did the hunters move on?

Where did they go?

With no communities, following the big game with their tiny projectiles, they left no mark of their presence. Where did their bones go?

Did the climate get warmer in mid-America and a new people develop who did not come from anywhere?

There are questions.

In 1949 with the use of carbon 14, excavations in Clovis, New Mexico, changed the picture of the mound builders' background. The setting back of time by the carbon 14 tests has brought into question the idea of man coming across a land bridge from another country. Some believe now that North America was the home of primordial, indigenous American man who inhabited the middle area of the country.

The new dating places the occupation of all the Americas at an earlier time than was thought, and gives rise to amazing new conjectures of the origins of these first and sometimes called lost Americans.

Archaeology, the study of ancient peoples, as a recognized science has developed meaningfully in the last century. The organized effort to appraise the magnificent cultures of the Maya, Aztecs, Totonacs, Olmecs, and mound builders of North America has taken place within the twentieth century. These discoveries have just begun. And it is this new questioning that has suggested that instead of looking to Europe or Asia for the first American, we look to South America and consider that he may have come up the down staircase instead of down the up.

Now scientists believe that a race of Americans might have developed in both North and South America that did not come

dark ancestors

from an old world culture or over any land continent, and did not develop from some other race.

In the old theories there may have been some hidden racism. These theories were created at the time when we were picturing Indians as vermin, a wall to our expansion, and we thought of them as hunters averse to labor, lazy and villainous. So we theorized that these industrious mound builders laboring in this vast construction could not have been related to the Indian who stubbornly obstructed our way to the conquest of the Americas.

But scientists with new machinery, the deeper digs made by road construction, as well as the protection of archaeological digs from wanton destruction, have made a new and exciting picture of what might have taken place when these mounds were built by some dark ancestors.

The new picture raises other questions.

It contradicts the model of the big-game hunter or even of the migrant with Mongolian strains coming overland from Asia. And all this questioning and setting back of time seems to indicate some movement of glaciers and the coming of warmth over the mid-country.

Is it possible that a race of people can come up from "below," as the Indian says, out of the warming weather after the glacial period, out of the phenomenon of rising earth, abundant with food growing from coast to coast, wild and free? Can such a race arise from a multiple environment of a continent?

An archeological dig at Mound City.
The shallow holes are believed
to have been a line of posts.

At some period the big mammoths, the mastodon, the saber-tooth cat, the great bison disappeared, were snuffed out, possibly by some change of weather. (There is a modern — but different — species of bison existing today.) The shift from hunting to food gathering was made possible by the melting of the glaciers. With the rising of the oceans and the effect of summer being felt all over the continent, flora and fauna returned. These foragers and gatherers probably never ate a mammoth steak in their lives. They filled the prairies and both ocean shores, Atlantic and Pacific. We cannot assume they were one people. There were 2,200 languages in North America alone when the white man came.

There must have been great diversity. A single movement of people seems unlikely. The land began to feed them from coastal lowlands to the desert.

These must have been quite different people from the big-game hunters. These people who were food gatherers, berry pickers, ate their way through long summers into the great middle country, along the coasts of the Pacific and Atlantic where, after the glacier periods, they could gather food.

Oyster beds have been found on the Atlantic coast where there was no salt water in our span of history. Abundance made

food gatherers—flower people

it possible to stay in one place a full season or to stop and raise a family, and finally to settle.

Instead of living in bands of ten to fifteen persons like the mammoth hunters, taking cover in the long winters in some cave, they were able to build stable centers like the places where they built mounds. The game hunters, because of their hard existence, could not advance their tribe more than two or three people every hundred years. Now many people began to be seen along the Mississippi River and it was probably at this time that they began to make cemeteries, bury their dead, remember their grandparents, and build memorial structures.

The roving bands of men and women began to multiply and filled the Americas north and south from the Arctic Circle to Land's End with a new people. In this temperate environment a civilization was nurtured. Users of the fruits of the earth populated the river valleys.

Perhaps they learned to preserve food, digging and drying roots and fruits, families meeting and celebrating and staying and building mounds where they picnicked. They had time to improve their pebble, stone, and chopper tools, or they learned other methods of obtaining food such as pounding acorns to flour.

By the Mississippian period (c. 700 A.D. — 1700 A.D.) they were farmers.

Four major groups of mound builders and the times in which they flourished were the Poverty Point culture (c. 1,000 B.C.) found in Louisiana, the Adena culture (c. 1,000 B.C. — 500 A.D.) in Ohio, the Hopewellian culture (400 B.C. — 900 A.D.) in Illinois and also in Ohio, and the Mississippian culture (700 A.D. — 1700) which spread from the Ohio and Tennessee valleys into an area that stretched from South Carolina to Texas and from Wisconsin to Florida.

Their culture names merely indicate where the first excavations were made. While the mound culture spread from Iowa to the border of the Great Lakes, to the eastern forests and through Georgia and Florida, the major concentration was in the areas of Illinois, Ohio, and Mississippi.

The cultures were alike in some ways, but there were also differences. The Poverty Point people were nearer to the culture of South America. Their high pyramids were not only for the burial of their dead but may also have been monuments to the sun and moon where they held elaborate rituals marking the seasons.

The Adena culture had the most elaborate cult of the dead. The Hopewellian had long heads, and were more aggressive than the Adena culture although they lived side by side for many

the dead and the living

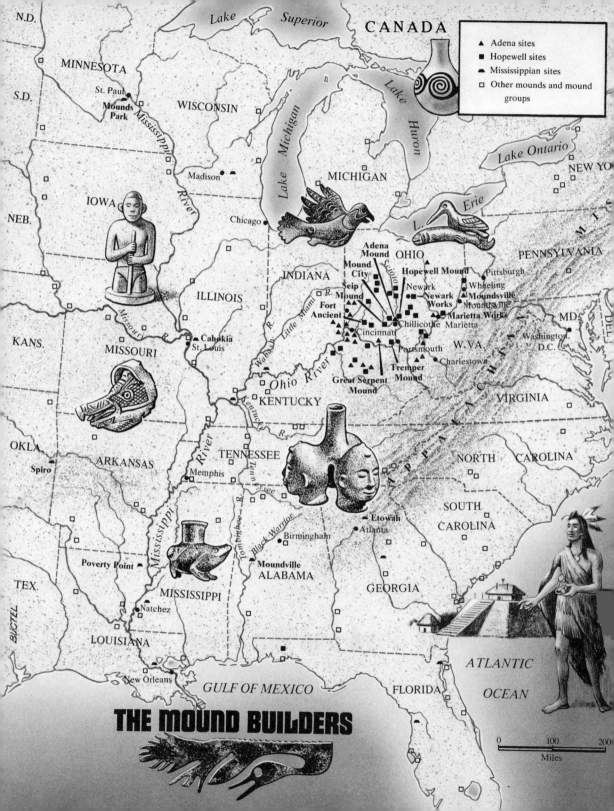

N.D.

S.D.

MINNESOTA

Lake Superior

CANADA

- ▲ Adena sites
- ■ Hopewell sites
- ◣ Mississippian sites
- ☐ Other mounds and mound groups

St. Paul
Mounds Park

WISCONSIN

Lake Michigan

Lake Huron

Lake Ontario

NEW YO

NEB.

IOWA

Madison

MICHIGAN

L. Erie

PENNSYLVANIA

MTS.

Chicago

Mississippi River

Missouri River

KANS.

MISSOURI

Cahokia
St. Louis

ILLINOIS

INDIANA

Wabash R.

Little Miami R.

R.

Adena Mound

OHIO

Mound City

Seip Mound

Fort Ancient

Cincinnati

Scioto R.

Hopewell Mound

Newark

Newark Works

Chillicothe

Marietta

Pittsburgh

Wheeling

Moundsville

Marietta Works

MD.

Washington, D.C.

DEL.

OKLA

Spiro

ARKANSAS

Memphis

Mississippi River

Kentucky R.

TENNESSEE

Tennessee R.

KENTUCKY

Ohio River

Portsmouth

Tremper Mound

Great Serpent Mound

W. VA.

Charlestown

VIRGINIA

APPALACHIAN MTS.

NORTH CAROLINA

TEX.

Poverty Point

BUCTEL

LOUISIANA

Natchez

MISSISSIPPI

Tombigbee R.

Black Warrior R.

Moundville

ALABAMA

Birmingham

Atlanta

Etowah

SOUTH CAROLINA

GEORGIA

New Orleans

GULF OF MEXICO

FLORIDA

ATLANTIC OCEAN

THE MOUND BUILDERS

0   100   200
Miles

centuries. They were merchants who traveled the rivers with their wares, exchanged raw materials, went south as far as Mexico and west to the Rockies. They were skillful craftsmen and artists.

The Mississippian culture is the only one whose mounds were specifically constructed as temples, although they may also have served burial purposes. Craftsmanship reached a high level in the Mississippian groups. Many beautiful artifacts — statues, masks, and jewelry — have been found in their mounds.

The mounds of Poverty Point along the Mississippi River in Louisiana were first mentioned in a Smithsonian Institute report in 1872. They were not examined until fifty years later, when Clarence B. Moore saw them from a steamboat. It was not until the 1950s when aerial photos revealed their vastness that they were closely studied. Scientists then observed their immense size and geometric arrangement of concentric octagons. The largest was 700-800 feet at the base, rising 70 feet above the surrounding plain, estimated to have taken three million man-hours of labor to build.

It is thought that, unlike the Adena mounds, these were built in a single effort and inhabited at the same time by an organized community. The carbon date — 1200 B.C. — is older than that of the Adena mounds.

At Poverty Point six low ridges form half an octagon three-quarters of a mile across. The seventy-foot mound is in the center, and other mounds in the surrounding area. There was once a set of six concentric octagons. The total length of the ridges was at one time over eleven miles. The mound had a mass over thirty-five times that of the Cheops pyramid in Egypt.

Poverty Point was probably the ceremonial center of the culture of that time. Six sites might have belonged to this culture with influence as far north as Indiana. With Adena occupying

poverty point's great pyramids

the upper Ohio Valley and Poverty Point the lower Mississippi Valley, they may have encountered each other on the trade routes along the river.

There are thirty-two sites with Poverty Point traits and others that may have been related. They are believed to date from about 1200 to 100 B.C. The clustering of towns makes it seem that Poverty Point was the center of the culture group. It must have been very archaic since they had no pottery, not even pots for cooking purposes. Curious relics are the millions of round clay mud balls that have been found. They are the size of snowballs as if made in the cupped hand. With not a rock within miles, these are cooking stones made to drop into the cooking baskets or to lay on coals. They may have held a special flavor like charcoal as they seem to have been thrown away and new ones made.

The culture may have developed from an ancient hunting base and, because of the natural tropical growth, become a center for the gatherers and then for more permanent settlements.

Of the incredible center of this culture only about half remains today, but what is left leaves us amazed by its beauty, symmetry, and complexity. The two mounds which remain may have supported a temple.

You can imagine gatherings of people coming up and down the rivers in their bright clothes, walking the geometric paths which possibly imitated the configuration of the stars. The octagon aisles would be massed with huge assemblages to celebrate the seasons, fires burning, thousands dancing, and the priests on the temples at the apex blessing the wide land.

We say they disappeared. Actually, there probably was no break between the mound builders and the Indians as we now know them. The Indians do not tell us their memories but they keep them alive within themselves.

The Adena culture seems to have originated in the eastern woodlands sometime around 1,000 to 800 B.C., developing slowly into a food gathering group centered around Chillicothe, Ohio, on the Scioto River. Its sphere of influence spread through the Ohio Valley for 150 miles and remains of it have been found even in West Virginia and Kentucky.

The culture of the Adena was built on the honored dead. Their mounds were funeral mounds, cemeteries for the dead, before the mounds became temples. They are conical and seem to have been built up gradually from the burial of one or two people. They grew by accretion to tremendous size and the temples were probably built on the tops of them.

The contents of the mounds show the deepening and enriching of the burial cult of the honored dead. As the bodies lay in state, they were surrounded with what was precious to them in life and what they would need for the journey of death. Their bodies were painted with red graphite or ochre. Small bowls filled with food were near at hand. They are similar to the Aztec bowls with their flowing lines. Tablets with designs of abstract forms of animals and birds — hawks, eagles, vultures — were discovered, as well as awls and grinding stones.

There are altars where it is clear that cremation, the burn-

adena mounds of the dead

ing of bodies, took place. Special burial places of priests, chiefs, or other important people have also been found, containing rich artifacts of copper breastplates, obsidian masks, and other objects.

One of the artifacts found in the Adena Mound in Ohio has given us a picture of what the individual Adena looked like. It is a red and yellow clay effigy pipe in the shape of a squat male figure, although he was apparently suffering from diseases. He has a strong face, an elaborate headdress, and wears ear spools similar to those found in effigies in Yucatan.

They seem to have been a sober, religious people who held their nation together a long time in the interstices of Hopewellian culture. We do not know whether they were tolerated or despised, or whether the cultures mingled together. We do know that they were contemporaries for over nine hundred years.

The Adena relics along the Ohio mark a religious center. A community of holy ground must have developed around the mounds which supported a priesthood and a religion.

We take burying of the dead for granted, but we have to imagine what it was to conceive of stopping to bury the dead, interrupting the great food-gathering trek for this purpose. Burying of the dead indicates to some extent the development of the individual. Burial is a social act. Burial mounds mean a tribute, memory, respect to individuals.

Skeletal remains have been found surrounded by the

The Adena pipe, a clay pipe
in the shape of a man wearing
a headdress and ear spools.

The Great Serpent Mound,
Adams County, Ohio.

ancient pollen of the flowers mounded upon the dead. These early men had become human enough to believe in individual personality and to hope for continuation after death. Perhaps they first started ceremonial burial in caves, laying the dead under a stone or in a cave sealed with rocks.

Possibly when they ran out of caves, they began to bury their dead, and built up the mounds slowly, starting with one grave and building up mound after mound, some hardly a foot high and others reaching a height of seventeen feet. They seem to have built their mounds over hundreds of years, repeated burials mounting them up.

Most of the Adena mounds are conical, all but the famous Great Serpent Mound, the largest snake effigy in the world, found in Adams County, Ohio. Here you see a low, mounded, rounded bank nearly a quarter of a mile long, showing a gigantic serpent in the act of uncoiling. The head of the serpent lies above a rock precipice a hundred feet above the waters of Brush Creek; it has seven coils that writhe southward to a triple coiled tail. In what appears to be the open mouth of the serpent is an oval form, thought by some to represent a frog, but which seems more likely to be an egg.

From head to tail the serpent is 1,254 feet in length and in width about 20 feet. The mound that forms it is 4 or 5 feet high. The open jaws are 75 feet apart.

Almost destroyed in the last century, it is awesome today. On a summer day hundreds of people swarm over this ancient effigy. It is now a public park covered with green grass with an observation tower from which one can look down and try to imagine the ancient meaning.

The Hopewellian culture is named for a site in Ross County, Ohio, where excavations of this group were first made. Carbon 14 dates it as sometime before 1000 A.D. Some say these people entered from the woodlands and penetrated the Adena culture. They must have been neighbors, as we have mentioned, for nine hundred years or more.

Although the two cultures existed at one time and within miles of each other, the Hopewellian culture was of a different nature. They might be called the first empire builders. They were merchants, engineers, artists, architects. They went up and down the river trading and teaching. Wherever they went, they were picturesque and of great influence.

From a central area of government buildings around Chillicothe, Ohio, the influence of the Hopewellian people extended across what is now Indiana, Illinois, Wisconsin, and Michigan. Remains have been found as far south as Mississippi. Their range was enormous. They sent out traders, exchanged raw materials and manufactured objects, and brought back copper from Upper Michigan, mica from the Appalachians, flints and obsidian from as far west as the Rockies. Also they had conch shells from the Gulf Coast, grizzly bear teeth, silver, and iron.

hopewell merchants of america

*A copper artifact of
the Hopewellian culture.*

People in great numbers probably came to their seasonal ceremonials, fairs, and gatherings. The oldest of their mounds at Fort Ancient consists of colossal geometric earth ramparts and avenues leading from the Little Miami River. The enclosures of Newark in southern Ohio are most imposing, once covering four miles of long parallel earth avenues now gone, but the remaining great circle, with walls fourteen feet high, is now an enormous fairground. At the center is a great eagle mound. These construction projects, geometric earth ramparts and pyramids, were more than burial mounds.

The Newark earthworks have been compared to Stonehenge in England, or Carnac in Brittany, France. The builders possessed standards of measurement and had some means of determining an angle. Skillful engineers of our time would find it difficult without the aid of instruments to lay down an accurate square or circle. The circle is four-fifths of a mile in circumference. These mounds seem to have been built differently from the Adena burial mounds. Inside them there are ramps, rooms, and tunnels.

At Mound City, near Chillicothe, Ohio, there is a group of some twenty-four mounds, the highest of which is almost eighteen feet high. In these mounds, beginning in the nineteenth century, clay pipes were found, skillfully carved in the shapes of animals and birds. On this site, explorers also found masks and copper figures.

Despite the spoliation of these mounds by treasure seekers, the wealth found in them shows a civilization rich in materials, in design, in engineers and craftsmen, and above all, in wandering merchants who brought back the riches of the continent. The Hopewell people's generosity in placing such quantities of goods in their burial mounds puzzles scientists: how did they acquire this wealth?

Pages 38-42:
the Mound City group in Ohio.

The Seip Mound is in size the second largest of the Hopewell mounds. In one grave was found a skeleton covered from head to foot with river pearls. In a vault four adults and two infants were found also covered with pearls and ornaments of copper, mica, tortoise-shell, and silver. A skull was found with an artificial nose of copper. (The nearest known source of copper is Michigan.)

Not only burial artifacts were found in the Hopewell mounds but the creative wealth of an artistic community.

Silver also was found; it must have come from the Southwest. There were profusions of ivory, as well as fossil teeth, sculptures of coiled serpents like the Aztec gods, scrolls of mica, bone needles, exquisite carved pipe ornaments, copper axes, and spool-shaped ear ornaments.

In some vaults tall young men and women lie side by side in barbaric splendor, copper encircling their skeletons, breastplates on their breasts, all showing the care and skill of the Hopewellian artisans.

*Left: a pottery head from
the Seip Mound in Ohio.
Above: a platform pipe from
the Mound City group.*

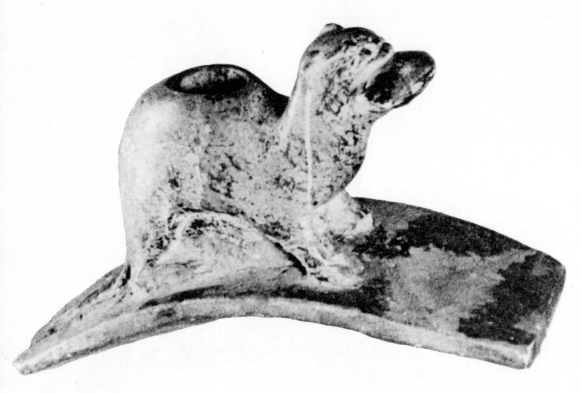

*Above: a pipe in the shape
of an otter with a fish
in its mouth from the
Tremper Mound in Ohio.
Right: a human effigy in copper
from the Mound City group.*

The Mississippian group of mound builders followed after the Hopewell people with a lapse of a few centuries in between. The Mississippians represent the last flare of elaborate North American mound building. After 1200 A.D. the Mississippian culture, which had developed in the Mississippi Valley about five hundred years before, spread out in many directions and their mounds are found in a widespread area concentrated in Illinois, Missouri, Arkansas, and Tennessee, but also stretching as far east as Georgia, as far north as southern Minnesota, and as far west as eastern Texas.

The mounds are unusual in that they were constructed as temples of worship rather than primarily for burial purposes. The northern Mississippians built conical mounds. The mounds of the southern Mississippians are rectangular with flat tops that served as the bases for the wooden temples and other structures, such as chiefs' huts, that were built on top of them.

The great size of the temple mounds has impressed all who have studied them. The Cahokia Mound (also called Monks' Mound because a group of monks once cultivated vegetables on top of it) in Madison County, Illinois, is of colossal size: one hundred feet high, sixteen acres in expanse — the largest North American mound in terms of volume. The large Cahokia Mound

the artistic mississippians

is surrounded by a series of smaller mounds; there may have been up to one hundred of these smaller mounds, but only forty have been preserved. This mound group is believed to date from about 1400 to 1600 A.D.

The Etowah Mounds in northern Georgia are another tremendous group. There are three mounds at Etowah; the largest, a pyramid with a flat top, covers almost three acres. These, like all mounds, were built of earth, carried, probably in baskets or pieces of cloth, by individuals working without tools or equipment. Occasionally a basket, dropped by a worker, has been found encased in the dirt of a mound.

The Mississippian mounds have yielded a rich harvest of artistic works, including copper plaques, pottery, and stone statuary. The artifacts are frequently embellished with elaborate designs, and what are probably religious cult symbols. Weeping eyes, fighting cocks, and rattlesnakes are repeated subjects.

From the impressive accomplishments of construction and artistic design they had achieved, the Mississippian culture faded out, until by the time the Spanish arrived on the American continent there were only weak remains of the temple mound people.

Left: two scenes from
Indian Mounds Park in
St. Paul, Minnesota.
Page 52: a stone figure of the
Mississippian culture from
the Duck River in Tennessee.
Page 53: a shell pendant with
a rattlesnake design of the
Mississippian culture from
Chickamauga Creek, Tennessee.

The mound builders made monuments of grand design. They were not merely useful as burial places; there is some reason for thinking some of them were fortresses used as defense against enemies. They were not mere breastworks.

The Mississippian culture died out. Hopewellians were also gone before the invasion from Europe. The Adenas disappeared. The Poverty Point people left their pyramids and villages which were later occupied by the Creeks, the Caddoes, and the Chickasaws.

Where did they go?

What caused an entire culture to fade away without trail or footprint, allowing their temples to fall into ruins, leaving a country endeared to them by long residence and labor?

They disappeared sometime, somewhere.

Was there a change in climate? Was there a drought? Corn is subject to pestilence. Did it in one year die out? Perhaps a powerful group seized the mound builders, exacted high taxes, oppressed the people in some way. But they had no known enemies. They were not warriors. There are no caches of weapons. They were not aggressive empire builders. The use of the mounds as fortresses, though, would indicate a defense against enemies.

the silent heritage

When the white man entered the interior of the continent in the sixteenth century, he found the plains and the prairie Indian with little wealth but corn. The mound building Indians were just about gone. Did the modern Indian as we know him conceal and hide the great culture, fearful of its destruction even in memory?

White men found the Shawnees near Chillicothe but they were shut out by the Indians from any knowledge of continuity of history. Grass and forest shrubbery grew over the mounds and their age was marked only by trees grown over the holy dead. What was left of the ghosts of the great civilization withered at the white man's touch.

Fleeting ghostly evidences of the old race appear in the ball game the Caddoes play, or when an old man tells that the mounds represented the navel of the earth, the center, and then is silent.

The greedy have looted the contents of the mounds, plowed up the burial grounds. Bulldozers have sheared them away to make highways. Tourists, pot hunters, thieves still dig them up. In Oklahoma vandals dynamited the mounds and poured out ashes from decorated containers, destroying valuable historical evidence.

Golfers play over the sites of the old temples in Ohio. Roads for tourists lead to the top in Illinois. A tower has been built over the Great Serpent Mound. Mining companies have mined through the corridors of the dead.

But governments are now trying to preserve the mounds as parks, and before highways are built scientists are invited to excavate the sites.

Ceram, C. W. *The First American*. New York: Harcourt Brace Jovanovich, 1971.

Farb, Peter. *Man's Rise to Civilization*. New York: E. P. Dutton, 1968.

Hibben, Frank C. *Digging Up America*. New York: Hill and Wang, 1960.

Silverberg, Robert. *The Mound Builders of Ancient America*. Greenwich, Conn.: New York Graphic Society, 1968.

Ronan, John. "Resurrection in Illinois," *Saturday Review*, November 25, 1972 (*Saturday Review*, *Science*, December 1972).

Stuart, George. "Mounds: Riddles from the Indian Past," *National Geographic*, December, 1972.

bibliography

Adena culture, 23-25, 27, 29-33
    art, 29
        burial mounds at Chilli-
           cothe, 3, 29, 30-33
        pottery, 29
Animal effigies, 1, 2, 29, 37
Antler artifacts, 2, 5
Apes, 14
Archaeology, 17
Architects, 35
Art:
      Adenian, 29
      Hopewellian, 5, 43
      Mississippian, 25, 51
Atlantis, 11
Axes, 5, 14, 43
Aztecs, 5, 17, 29

Baily, Francis, 11
Baskets, 2, 28, 51
Behemoth, 11
Bering Strait, 6, 12

Bird effigies, 1, 2
Bison, 14, 21
Bone artifacts, 2, 5, 43
Breastplates, 5, 30, 43
Burial mounds, 5
      Adenian, at Chillicothe, 3
       29, 30-33
      cremation, 5, 29-30
      Hopewellian, 37, 43
      Poverty Point culture, 3
      robbers of, 3, 11, 37, 56

Caddoe Indians, 55
Cahokia mounds, 2, 3, 49, 51
Cahokia Mounds State Park,
    Ill., 2
Carbon 14 dating process, 17
Carnac, France, 37
Carvings, 5, 37. *See also*
    Statues
Ceremonial centers, 3, 27, 37.
    See also Temple mounds

index

Ceremonies, 2, 28, 37
Cheops pyramid, Egypt, 27
Chickasaw Indians, 55
Chiefs, 5, 30, 49
Chillicothe, Ohio, 3, 29, 35, 37
Choppers, stone tools, 14, 22
Cloth, 2, 5, 28
Clovis, New Mexico, excavations at, 14, 17
Clovis points, 14
Copper:
    artifacts, 30, 37, 43, 51
    traded, 5, 35
Crafts, 25, 37. *See also* Baskets; Jewelry; Masks; Pottery
Creek Indians, 55
Cremation, 5, 29-30

Dance, 2, 28
Dating, carbon 14 method, 17
Defense, 55
Donnelly, Ignatius, 11

Ear spools, 30, 43
Effigies, animal, 1, 2, 29, 33
Egyptian pyramids, 1, 27
Engineers, 35, 37
Eskimos, 15
Etowah mounds, 51
Evolution, 14
Excavations, 12, 14, 17, 23

Families, 22
Farming, 22
Flint points, 5, 14, 35
Flour, 22
Folsom flint points, 14
Food, 14, 21, 22
Foragers, food, 5, 21-22
Fort Ancient, 37
Fortifications, 55
Fossil teeth, 43
Fruits, 22
Funeral mounds, 5
    Adenian, at Chillicothe, 3, 29, 30-33
    cremation, 5, 29-30
    Hopewellian, 37, 43
    Poverty Point culture, 3
    robbers of, 3, 11, 37, 56

Gatherers, food, 5, 21-22
Geographic distribution, mounds, 1, 23
Glaciers, 12, 19, 21
Grave robbers, 3, 11, 37, 56
Great Serpent Mound, 2, 12, 33

Headdresses, 5
Hopewellian culture, 3, 23, 35-43
    art, 5, 43
    burial mounds, 37, 43

pottery, 5, 11, 37
trade, 5, 35, 37
Hunters, 19, 21, 22, 28
Paleo, 14-15

Indians, 1, 19, 28
Instruments, musical, 2
Iron, traded, 35
Israelite tribe of Dan, 11
Ivory artifacts, 43

Jefferson, Thomas, 12
Jewelry, 5, 25, 43

Knives, flint, 14

Language, 21
Lapidary art, 5

Magic. *See* Religion
Mammoths, 14, 21, 22
Masks, 25, 37
Obsidian, 2, 5, 30
Mastadons, 21
Maya, 17
Mica, artifacts, 5, 35, 43
Migration, 6, 11-15, 17-19
Mississippian culture, 23, 25, 49-51
art, 25, 51
pottery, 51

Monk's Mound, 49, 51
Monuments, 23, 55
Moon ritual, 23
Moore, Clarence B., 27
Mound City, 37
Mounds:
construction, 2, 37
destruction of, 3, 11, 56
preservation of, 56
temple, 2, 25, 49, 51
See also Burial mounds
Music, 2

Nomads, 14, 21, 22

Obsidian, 35
jewelry, 5
masks, 2, 5, 30
Origin, mound builders, 6, 11-15, 17-19

Paleo hunters, 14-15
Pearls, 5, 43
Pipes, 30, 37, 43
Pottery:
Adenian, 29
Hopewellian, 5, 11, 37
Mississippian, 51
Poverty Point culture, 28
Poverty Point culture, 23, 27-28

burial mounds, 3
pottery, 28
trade, 28
Priests, 3, 28, 30
Pyramids, 1, 2, 3, 27. *See also* Mounds

Reincarnation, 33
Religion, 3, 23, 28, 30, 33, 49, 51
River travel, 6, 12, 25

Sabertooth cat, 21
Sculpture, 43. *See also* Statues
Seasons, celebration of, 23, 28, 37
Seip Mound, 43
Sepulchre vaults, 3. *See also* Burial mounds
Serpents, sculptures, 43
Shamans, 3, 28, 30
Shawnee Indians, 56
Shells, 5, 35, 43
Silver artifacts, 5, 35, 43
Skeletons, 30, 43
Skulls, 14, 43
Smithsonian Institute, 27
Social rank, 5

Spear points, 14. *See also* Flint points
Statues, 25, 37, 51
Stone artifacts, 5, 51
Stone tools, 22. *See also* Axes; Choppers; Flint points; Knives
Stonehenge, England, 37
Sun ritual, 23

Teeth, fossil, 43
Temple mounds, 2, 25, 49, 51
Temples, 1, 3, 25, 28, 49
Tools, 3, 5, 14, 22, 43. *See also* Axes; Choppers; Flint points; Knives
Tortoiseshell, 43
Totonacs, 17
Tower of Babel, 11
Trade, 25, 28
Hopewellian, 5, 35, 37
Turtle shells, 5

Weapons, 14. *See also* Flint points
Wisconsin glacier, 12

Meridel Le Sueur
has taught at the
University of Minnesota
and done historical research
on a grant from the
Rockefeller Foundation.
Born in Iowa, she now
lives in Albuquerque
and travels extensively
in Mexico. Mrs. Le Sueur
is the author of
North Star Country
and Conquistadores.

about the author